HOW TO HAVE FEMINIST SEX

A Fairly Graphic Guide

Flo Perry

PARTICULAR BOOKS

an imprint of

PENGUIN BOOKS

PARTICULAR BOOKS

UK | USA | Canada | Ireland | Australia
India | New Zealand | South Africa

Particular Books is part of the Penguin Random House
group of companies whose addresses can be found at
global.penguinrandomhouse.com

First published 2019
001

Printed in Italy by L.E.G.O. S.p.A.

A CIP catalogue record for this book is a
available from the British Library

ISBN: 978-024-139156-3

www.greenpenguin.co.uk

MIX
Paper from
responsible sources
FSC® C018179

Penguin Random House is committed to a
sustainable future for our business, our readers
and our planet. This book is made from Forest
Stewardship Council® certified paper.

To all my lovers, past and future
xoxoxoxox

A LITTLE BIT ABOUT ME

Hi, I'm Flo, and I've written a book about sex and feminism. My qualifications include being an emotionally well-adjusted slag and being really good at drawing boobs. I'm "extremely" bisexual. I say extremely because I fancy nearly all humans over 5'8" and some short ones too.

I live in East London with two housemates and a terrible cat.

I've had long-term relationships with both men and women. I'm currently on Hinge, Tinder and Feeld, so it's a miracle I get anything else done.

INTRODUCTION

Feminism is so IN right now. Forever 21 are selling T-shirts with stuff like "feminist babe" on them, and brands are all over International Women's Day, which is fab.

But our sex lives often remain as unexamined and as full of sexist bullshit as they were decades ago.

Being a feminist in the bedroom is hard. Feminism is great, but it's not much of a turn on. Lots of women would rather be picked up by a man, thrown on the bed and dominated than give a lecture on equal rights before sex. And that's totally fine.

What's fine in the bedroom might not be acceptable in the boardroom!

As long as you know...

That your pleasure is as important as his, and if you let go of control it's because you want to in the context of the romantic encounter. That your body doesn't need his approval to be beautiful. That if you said no it would all stop. That sexual assault isn't just bad sex. That wanting sex doesn't make you less valuable. That not wanting sex doesn't make you a prude. And that pubes are sexy.

The problem is, we don't choose what we believe. Throughout our lives our parents, the media, our mates and school all plant beliefs in our heads that may or may not be true and helpful.

We can't help what beliefs we've been landed with, but we can re-examine our beliefs and decide which ones we want to keep and which we need to try to chuck out.

Hopefully, this book will help you choose which beliefs you need to bin, and maybe give you a few new ones that will help you have a more feminist sex life.

BODY IMAGE

Hating the way you look is not very fun. The majority of women have wished to change the way they look at some point in their life. This is because the media shows us only pictures of one type of women: The Slim White Lady™

I have a perfect minimalist kitchen and occasionally orgasm from eating low-fat yoghurt.

The Slim White Lady™ is then photoshopped so much that even other slim white ladies feel inferior to her. You do not need to look like The Slim White Lady™ to be beautiful, healthy or worthy. You are enough just as you are. Anyone who says otherwise is probably trying to get you to buy their yoghurt.

When you feel sexy you have better sex. If you're not worrying about your cellulite you're more likely to be in the moment, experiencing maximum pleasure. But to stop worrying about your body you have to put in a lot of effort. And it's hard.

Step 1: Forgive yourself for worrying about your body.

It's not my fault that I hate my cellulite. The whole world told me it was bad. I believed them even though they are wrong.

It's really hard not to listen to all the body-negative voices.

You need to evolve some body-positive, feminist, noise-cancelling headphones. And that takes a lot of energy.

Step 2: Tell yourself you're beautiful. Or, if you can't manage that, tell yourself you're fine. Start with something you feel like you can believe.

Step 3: Don't beat yourself up if you have a negative thought about your body.

Some people find it useful to remember that what we consider a "perfect body" is completely arbitrary and varies widely from culture to culture and throughout history.

For example, the Efik tribe in Nigeria traditionally see fatter women as more desirable. Brides-to-be try to gain weight. Thin or fat, trying to be a body shape you're not for your wedding day is something we could all go on a diet from.

In the Middle Ages in Britain the forehead was thought to be the most attractive part of a woman's body. Women would often pluck out all their eyebrows and eyelashes to accentuate their forehead.

And remember, in the early 2000s women across the Western world were advised to shape their eyebrows into little sperms. A tragedy.

What's hard to find is a society that celebrates a variety of body shapes and expressions of beauty, but we're working on it.

Social media is often a bad place for your body image. People post pictures of themselves from their most flattering angle, and YouTube couples never talk about how they didn't have sex for three months before they posted their big "shock breakup reveal" video. But it can be a positive place too: unlike traditional media and advertising, social media shows people of all body types if you know where to look for them. There are amazing women of every size and shape on Instagram posting fabulous photos of themselves.

If you hate your double chin, go and find someone who has one similar to yours and like all their pictures.

If you hate how hairy you are, go and find someone who makes their stubble sexy.

If you obsess over your stretch marks or cellulite, go and find someone who celebrates theirs.

If you wish you had a flat tummy, follow people who make their belly look amazing.

We tend to be kinder to strangers than we are to ourselves. Filling my feed with beautiful women of all shapes and sizes has really helped me; maybe it will help you too.

You are always loveable.

Difference is what makes us beautiful.

Being thinner won't automatically make you happier.

Learning to love your body takes work. You need to scrap all the beliefs that the world has told you about how you'll be happier if you have cheekbones, or a bigger butt, or no FUPA (that's a fat upper pussy area, Mum.)

Being fat isn't the opposite of being beautiful.

Cake could make you happier than a flat stomach

Your skin might never be perfect, but you can love it anyway.

Scars show what you've survived.

Use this space to list positive things about your body.

Absolutely no negatives! Try to fill the whole page. If you find it hard to believe you are beautiful, start with writing down things that feel nice, or make you happy in other ways.

_____

_____

_____

_____

_____

_____

_____

_____

_____

_____

_____

_____

_____

P.S. You are sexy, beautiful and full of life.

GETTING TO KNOW YOUR GENITALS

Not all women have a vagina. Many trans and intersex women cannot or choose not to have gender-affirming surgery. Also, not all people with vaginas are women. Gender is a spectrum and people with vaginas occur along the whole damn thing. This section on genitals will mainly focus on vaginas, because most women have vaginas and because vaginas themselves have been the subject of a lot of misogyny in our sex lives. While phalluses seem to have been worshipped in many ancient cultures, vaginas seem to mainly be the subject of Japanese horror films.

THE PENIS

For the three men who decided to read this book. Hello, welcome to the party! This is what I have to say on the penis: some men see having a good penis that behaves itself as the key to being good in bed, when in fact it has nothing to do with it. The magical thing about sex isn't a sticky thing going in a holey thing. It's two people exploring each other's bodies and getting pleasure from that. So it doesn't matter if you can't get super hard all the time, or your dick isn't very big, or you come quickly. What matters is communicating with your partner about both of your needs and desires and being open to whatever they have to say.

OK, now we can talk about **The Vagina!**

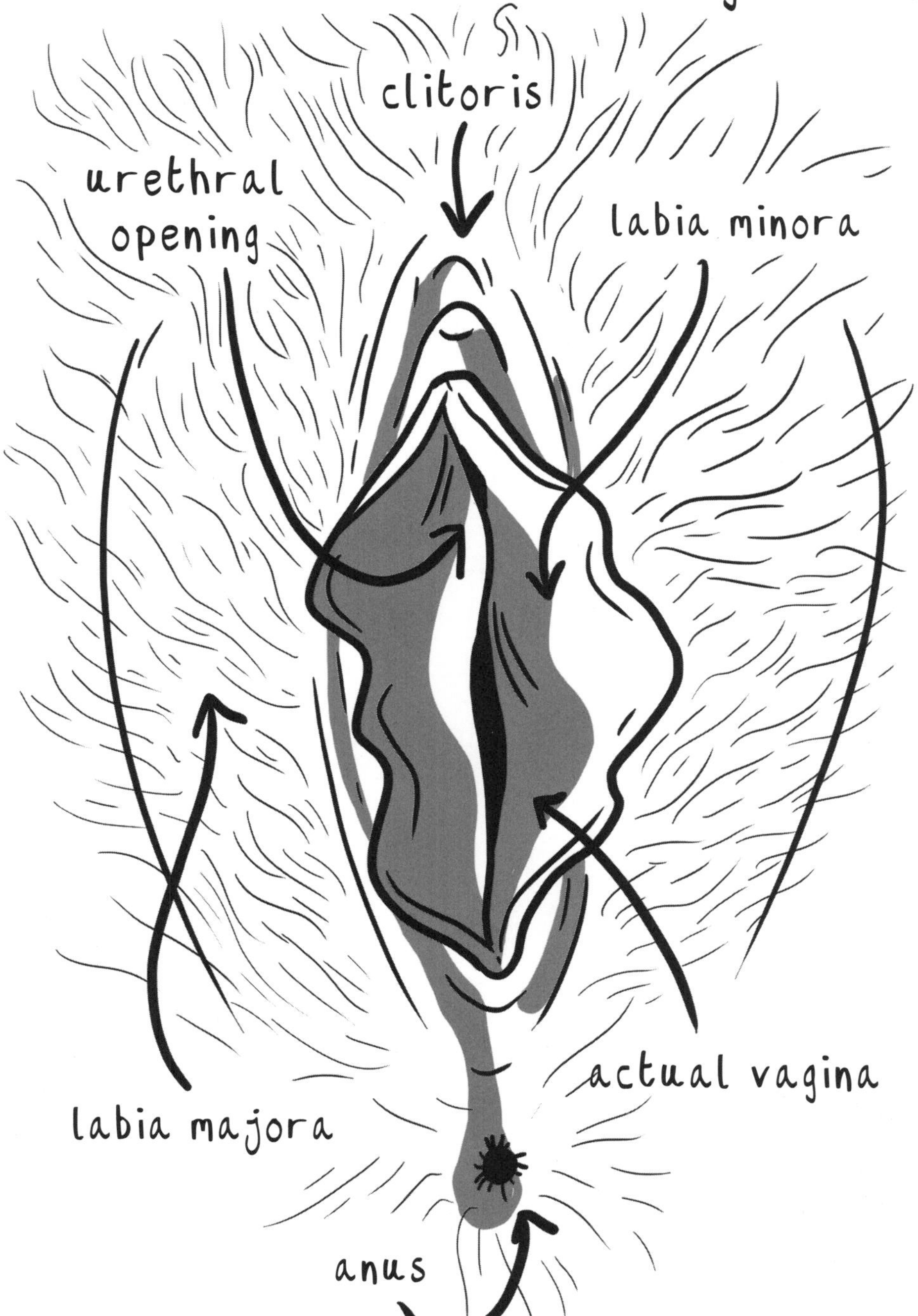
clitoris
urethral opening
labia minora
actual vagina
labia majora
anus

Most women will have all of these parts in their genitalia. Exactly how they look and what shape they are will vary wildly, but no version is superior to another.

Once upon a time, men would see only those vaginas they were about to have sex with. So they probably thought all vaginas were fucking fantastic. And then people started taking pictures of vaginas and putting them in magazines and, later, on this thing called "the internet". And suddenly the vagina had its own set of beauty standards and became another thing for women to feel bad about. Porn only shows one type of vagina. This has led to people without this type of vagina feeling like there is something wrong with them. That is crap. No type, shape or appearance of genitals is superior to any other. But it's easy for me to tell you to stop caring what your labia looks like; it's harder to actually stop. Remember that anyone who gets close enough to your vagina to know what your labia look like is going to be happy just to be invited.

ALL VAGINAS ARE BEAUTIFUL

There is no good word for describing female genitalia. "Vagina" only refers to the actual holey bit, but that's the term we use most often, and the one I will use throughout the book. "Vulva" is the technical term for the whole shebang, but it's a hard word to say without putting on a funny accent.

"Cunt" is a super fun word to say. It has shock value and it's punchy. But it's not exactly the word that female genitalia needs. Personally, I love that the most offensive word in the English langage means vagina. You can get away with saying dick in school, but cunt? That's serious.

I love my cunt.

I am neutral towards my twat.

"Twat" has lost its vagina-y meaning. It's mild, barely offensive, but not sexy or empowering either. It's a good thing to call your boss, but a crap thing to call your vagina.

I hate the word "pussy". Maybe you love it and it makes you feel sexy, in which case ignore me. If someone is a cunt they are ferocious, if someone is a pussy they are scared (which I think is an insult to both vaginas and cats). I think the kind of guy who says "pussy" wants to try those positions that only exist on Pornhub and will give you a slipped disc, but that might be just my experience.

PUBES

Why do women feel the need to remove their pubes?

Women's body hair is a political issue. It didn't ask to become one - it was just minding its fluffy business between your legs. But in the late 1980s to early 2000s, when women started ripping out their own pubes and men didn't follow suit, it became something that needs to be thought about. Why did we all start doing it?

What did I ever do to you?

Solidarity!

It was partly fashion, as our bikini lines rose and we started shaving, same as when our skirts got shorter and we shaved our legs. But that doesn't explain why many women these days feel compelled to pluck out every hair down there, even in winter. Or why women's body hair can't be seen in the first place.

It could be because female body hair is a sign of our own grown-up sexuality, and women having their own sexual desires that are separate from what a man wants is a scandalous concept.

It could be tied to the feminist movement in the 1970s. Women started showing their hair as a sign of rebellion against men, so men started fetishizing women without body hair. Perhaps the bedroom started being the only place men could be "men", and so they wanted to be the only ones with body hair.

It could be to do with the fact that the fetish for teenage girls went pretty mainstream in the 1990s with the publication of the porn magazine Barely Legal.

Whatever the reason, you can be pretty sure it's sexist, because millions of men aren't going to the beautician each month to have their arse crack waxed (though granted some are, good for them). And removing your pubes isn't fun. Some young men have never seen a full bush in the flesh, and some young women have never even seen their own full bush.

Do whatever you want with your pubes - they're yours to play with. But if you would like some guidance this might help...

The Pube Commandments

1) Pubes aren't digusting! It's not "cleaner" or more hygienic to have fewer pubes.

Actually, I reduce the risk of infection.

2) If anyone reacts negatively to your pubes, or cites your pubes as a reason not to give you oral sex, they are a knobhead.

Trust me, the bit you should focus on is bald

3) If anyone removes their pubes even though they don't like doing it, that doesn't make them a bad feminist. It's the patriarchy's fault; fighting the patriarchy is hard work, and sometimes you need to pick your battles.

4) At least once in your life, grow your bush to its full potential. For fun. For curiousity. For feminism. For laziness. For sex.

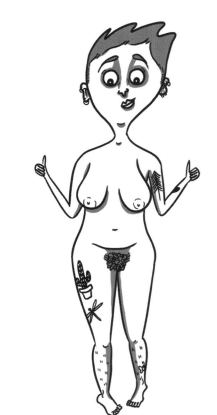

5) Always blowdry your pubes if you have the opportunity.

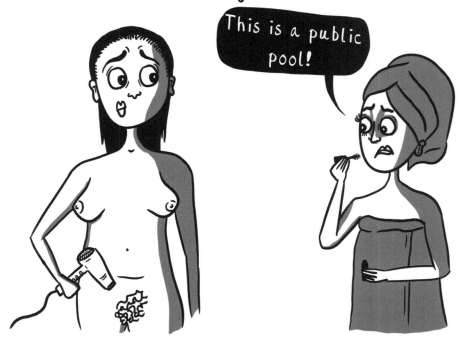

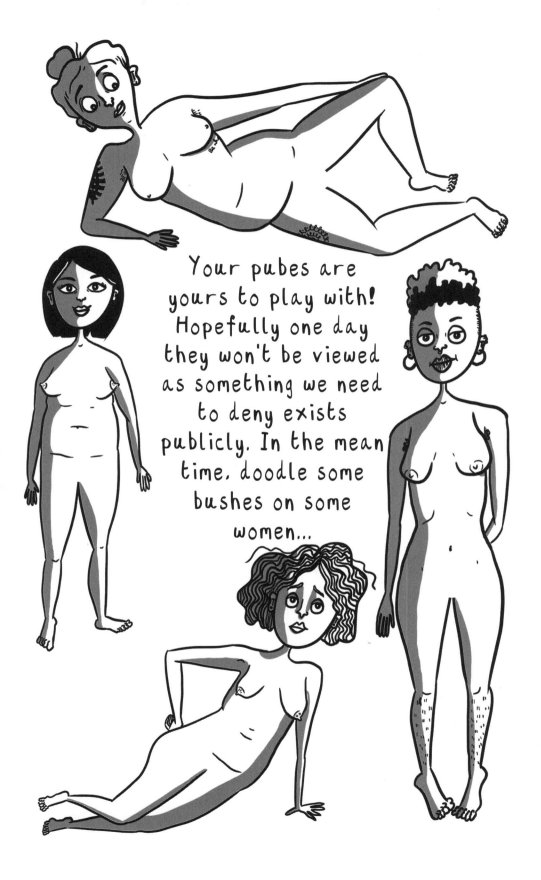

Your pubes are yours to play with! Hopefully one day they won't be viewed as something we need to deny exists publicly. In the mean time, doodle some bushes on some women...

DEALING WITH DISGUST

To enjoy sex, your brain has to overcome the part of itself that says, "You shouldn't touch other people's genitals, that's disgusting." Everyone has this part of their brain, which is a good thing: it makes the bus a more pleasant place to be.

But some people find it harder to get over this part of their brain. All sex is kind of disgusting and pretty unhygienic. But it's really fun, and whoever is going down on you is probably really loving it.

How is he doing that? Doesn't it smell bad?

Logically, we shouldn't want to lick each other's bumholes - it's where poo comes out, after all - but lots of us do it anyway. When we fancy someone, we forget about the fact that sex is gross. Some people even snog men with soul patches. Good for them.

VIRGINITY

It's a big ol' bag full of lies and myths.

Losing your virginity can feel like the most important thing that's ever going to happen to you, when in reality it's a bit of a non-event, much like your first chocolate croissant. Most people's first chocolate croissant was fine. It was probably from Sainsburys, and if you were lucky your mum would have shoved it in the microwave for 30 seconds first.

Thanks, Mum

What the fuck is this??

Some people's first chocolate croissant would have been bad, stale, disappointing, one of those bready ones that can last for a month.

A few people will have had the most amazing chocolate croissant in the world, straight out of the bakery in gay ol' Pareeee.

Mon Dieu!!

Sex is very different from pastry. But the point is that what your first chocolate croissant is like doesn't matter, because once you have discovered chocolate croissants you can have as many as you like and they will vary in quality wildly throughout your whole life.

Lots of people believe that virginity is a physical thing for people with vaginas. They believe that the hymen "breaks" when a vagina is penetrated for the first time, and that this is why some women bleed when they first have penetrative sex. In reality, the hymen is a membrane at the entrance to the vagina (not up inside but on the outside), with a flexible hole in it that rarely tears; and if it is damaged it can heal itself. There is no way of telling if someone has had penetrative sex or not by looking at their hymen.

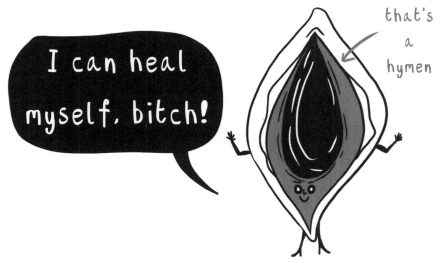

that's a hymen

I can heal myself, bitch!

Just like every other part of the body, hymens come in many shapes and sizes, and some people are even born without a hymen in the first place. Some people have a big hole in their hymen, some small, some several smaller holes.

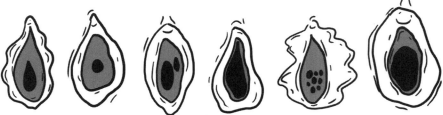

The hymen can become more flexible with penetration, and the first time it's stretched can be painful, but this isn't usually the main source of pain during sex. Over time, as our hormone levels change, so can our hymen, and many women's hymens shrink naturally over time.

The main source of bleeding and pain while losing your virginity is lack of lubrication. Which can be solved with the solution to most problems:* LUBE.

You can use lube on your first time! It might make it more enjoyable.

Virginity isn't a medical term, it's a social construct. And because of this, you get to decide when you've lost your virginity. Even the term "Lost your virginity" is fucked up. It's not something you can leave on the bus! You are in control of whether you identify as a virgin or not.

Has anyone seen my virginity?

I'm a virgin.

It's a meaningless term, so feel free to use it with abandon or not at all, until society accepts that you're not defined by your sexual history. I think everyone should be able to be a virgin.

*Disclaimer: lube is actually the solution only to a lack of lubrication during sex or to cleaning your dirty stainless-steel kitchen appliances. You're welcome.

Penetrative sex isn't some magic ceremony that you go through, leaving you somehow more enlightened afterwards.

It's just one type of sex on the smorgasbord of delightful sexual acts you can try.

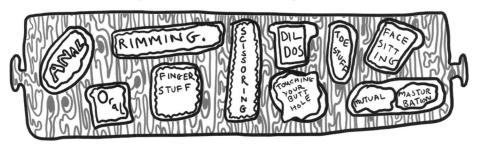

You don't have to have had penetrative sex to have lost your virginity, and if you have been penetrated it doesn't mean you can't say you're a virgin if you want to.

IT DOESN'T MATTER WHAT ANYONE ELSE THINKS ABOUT YOUR SEX LIFE

As women it can feel like we're constantly being ranked on a scale from "prude" to "slut", and that finding the exact right level of sexual desire and experience is the key to all happiness.

BEING A SLUT CAN BE FUN

Personally, I like the words "slut" and "slag". I've decided that in the sexpositive universe I have created for myself, being a slutty slaaaag can be a great thing - it just means you're being generous with your beautiful body.

But not everyone is as woke as me. For some reason, men can still get away with sleeping with more people than women do with less damage to their reputation.

Women have just as much potential as men to enjoy sex without emotional attachment. Not all sex has to be "meaningful". You can have a one-night stand you don't enjoy without it being the end of the world. You don't have to carry that regret with you. Sometimes, sleeping around can be amazing: it can boost your confidence and be one of the most exciting things life has to offer. Or it can be bad, and maybe you would have had more satisfaction from some cheesy chips. Or it can be shit, another reason you have to change your bedsheets.

You don't ever have to have a one-night stand

For some of us, sex can make us feel very emotionally close to the person we're having it with. We might want to be as sure as possible that it's safe for us to get emotionally attached to that person, that they'll stick around and treat us well. We might wait longer before we decide that we want to have sex with someone or not, to protect ourselves from hurt. This is totally valid and important.

Sometimes you know when this is gonna happen, sometimes you don't. You sleep with someone and afterwards it feels like your body won't stop craving them.

It can feel like your genitals have fallen in love with them. Suddenly they are all you can think about.

And sometimes you can have sex with someone and afterwards feel very little.

In my experience it is almost impossible to know which one of these is gonna happen. But what's important to remember is that this new relationship energy, where it feels like your body is in love with the person, doesn't last for ever, whether it is requited or not.

It is expected that men will want to shag as many people as they can and that women don't really like sex that much and only do it so we can trick a man into having babies with us. All genders have the potential to get emotionally attached after sex, or feel absolutely nothing. You can have a single one-night stand and decide they aren't for you, or you can have 20 and decide you're over them. Or you can think you want to wait until you are in a relationship and then one night say fuck it and meet someone you just wanna bang. Sex is super fun, and there's no point denying yourself because of made-up rules about what exactly is too many people to fuck. You and only you know when you want to shag someone. You still might make mistakes and get hurt. Humans are unreliable bastards and sex is messy. But you will survive.

Yeah... I'm not looking for a relationship right now....

You up?

Dental Dam

Silky LUBE xox

Did I leave my pants at yours?

The Ultimate One-Night Stand Guide

Mistakes I made so you don't have to

1) First of all, make sure you get very precise directions when going to the toilet in the middle of the night. Especially if their little brother is asleep downstairs.*

Five more minutes, Mum!

*Yes, this happened to me.

2) Only offer them breakfast if you have something to offer them for breakfast.

3) If you think you'll want to sneak out early, try to keep throwing your clothes around to a minimum.

4) Seriously, just use protection. And if you do get chlamydia don't take the meds before your own birthday party - they give you diarrhea.*

*Don't worry, it was only my friend's birthday party.

ORGASMS
What actually are they?

In short, an orgasm is a release of sexual tension.
But it is obviously so much more than that.
Sometimes, they are mind-blowingly pleasurable,
sometimes inconvenient, sometimes therapeutic, and
sometimes just like scratching an itch.

And they make your face
look like this

Orgasms for people with vaginas, and even very occasionally for people with penises, don't come with an obvious physical sign. There are things that often happen, for example contractions of the muscles around the vagina. But these don't always happen when a woman reports having an orgasm, and sometimes they happen without a woman having an orgasm.

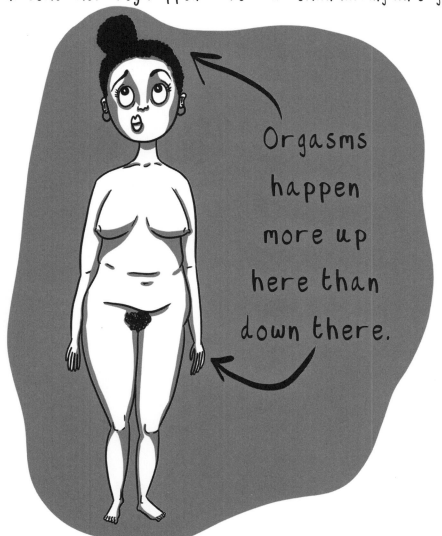

Orgasms happen more up here than down there.

In the same way that there is no way of telling if a woman is a virgin by looking at her vagina, there is no way of being sure whether a woman is having an orgasm or faking one. The only person who knows whether an orgasm is happening or not is the person having it (or not).

WHAT TO DO IF YOU'RE STRUGGLING TO HAVE AN ORGASM

If you really can't have an orgasm, don't worry. You can still have amazing sex without having one, and there are plenty of other things in life that are just as good and even better than orgasms. Nice food is better than orgasms. Hanging out with your friends is better than orgasms. Sitting on the sofa after a long walk is better than orgasms. Sometimes, the orgasm isn't even the best part of the sex: sometimes the best thing is seeing the person naked for the first time, or seeing the other person come; the excitement of doing it somewhere new, or learning just how sensitive your nipples are. So don't stress if you're not having any: it will be fine.

That said, they are pretty great. Not as good as your favourite food, but definitely better than your favourite series on Netflix. So if you can, and you want to, you should try to have them.

The enemy of orgasms is stress. If you're stressed about not having an orgasm, you probably won't have an orgasm. SO JUST RELAX... If only it were that easy. But really remember, orgasms aren't everything - you can have great sex without them.

If you've never ever had an orgasm, start by trying to have one on your own. That's right, I am talking about

MASTURBATION

If you've never tried masturbation, I really can't recommend it highly enough. It's fun, it relieves stress, it can help you sleep, and it's getting to know your body in the best way possible.

If you've never tried masturbation because you've been socially conditioned to think of it as disgusting, or morally wrong, or shameful, or that it will spoil sex with a partner for you, or that it will make you blind, I strongly advise that you let go of those beliefs, because they are bullshit. Replace them with the belief that masturbation can be a form of self-care.

If you've never had an orgasm before, set aside some uninterrupted time alone, at least 30 minutes, preferably an hour. Make sure you feel as safe and relaxed as possible. If you want to, you could do something that turns you on. This can be anything from just imagining scenarios that you find erotic, to watching porn, to reading your fave sex scene or some homoerotic Harry Potter fanfiction. Whatever floats your boat.

We can do whatever you want in your minnndddd.

Once you feel ready, find your clitoris. Do what feels good, and don't worry if you're doing it "right" or not. Stop if you want to, and try again another day. It doesn't matter if you don't orgasm. If you're having a nice time you've already reached the goal. Loads of teenagers hump pillows, spend a lot of time with the shower-head between their legs (god bless baths with shower-head attachments), or put their electric toothbrush where the sun don't shine for years before they actually have an orgasm.

If you're getting in your head and can't help pressuring yourself to orgasm, try masturbating while doing something else. Watch a movie, read a book, turn on the TV - it doesn't have to be sexy, it's just a way to let the mind drift - and see what happens.

If you get bored of doing this and it's not working for you, there are plenty of other techniques and resources, including loads of useful (vaguely office-safe) YouTube videos. If you want to try a vibrator, go for it. And even if you don't, I highly recommend reading some sex-toy reviews online because they are HILARIOUS.

★★★★★
Anon.

Bought the Bullet Vibe 1000 to spice up things between me and the wife, and let me tell you it did not disappoint. Battery life could be improved though.

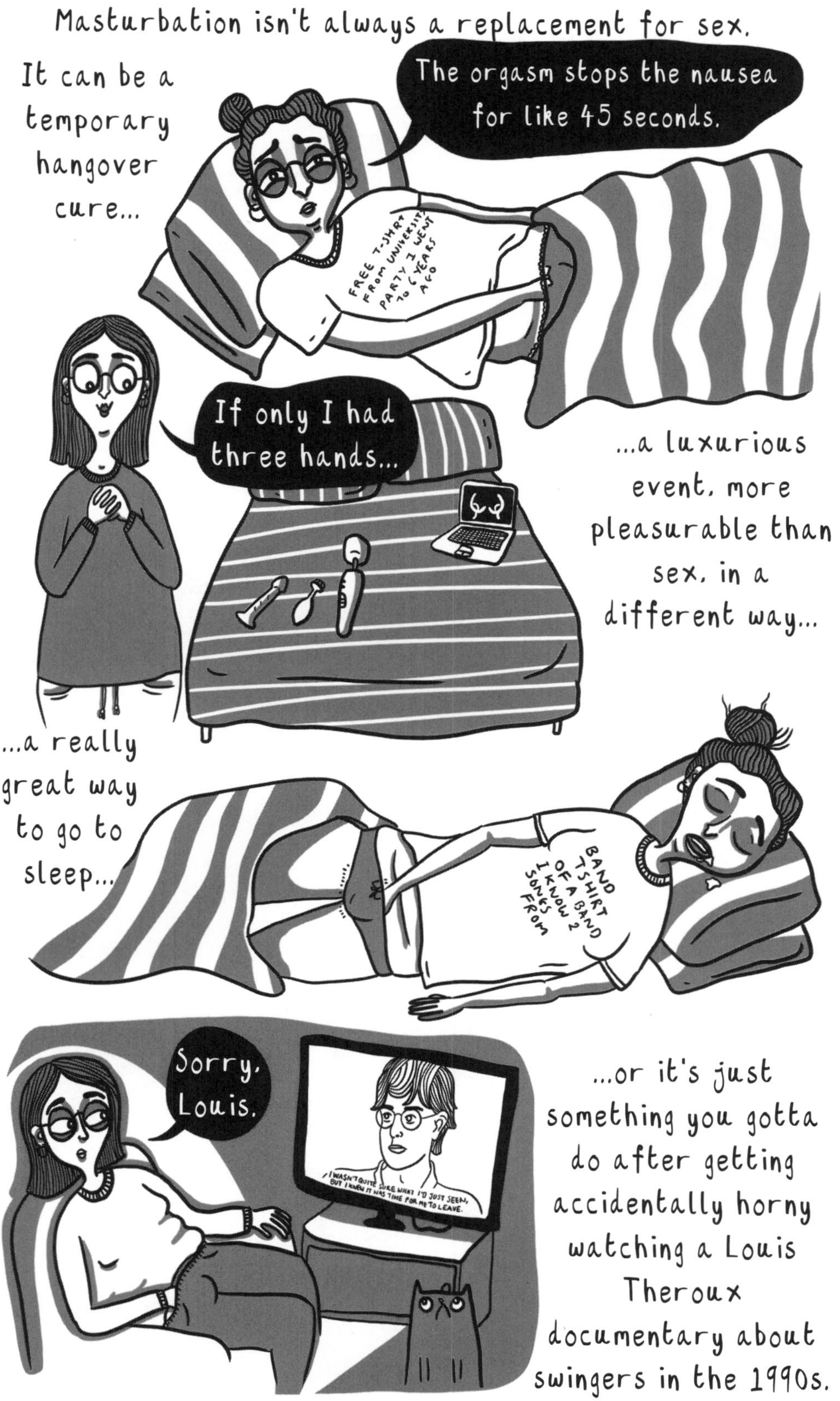
Masturbation isn't always a replacement for sex.
It can be a temporary hangover cure...
The orgasm stops the nausea for like 45 seconds.
FREE T-SHIRT FROM UNIVERSITY PARTY I WENT TO 6 YEARS AGO
If only I had three hands...
...a luxurious event, more pleasurable than sex, in a different way...
...a really great way to go to sleep...
BAND T-SHIRT OF A BAND I KNOW 2 SONGS FROM
Sorry, Louis.
I WASN'T QUITE SURE WHAT I'D JUST SEEN, BUT I KNEW IT WAS TIME FOR ME TO LEAVE.
...or it's just something you gotta do after getting accidentally horny watching a Louis Theroux documentary about swingers in the 1990s.

HAVING AN ORGASM WITH SOMEONE ELSE

What should you do if you orgasm reliably alone but struggle to orgasm with a partner? There are many, many reasons why this might happen, as every couple, sexual encounter and orgasm is a little bit different. But here are some general tips:

1) Stop trying to make orgasms the goal of sex.

Don't think of yourself as a failure if you or your partner don't orgasm during sex. Focus on the sex just being pleasurable. It can go on as long as you both want, or stop at any time. You don't need to achieve anything from it. Sex without an orgasm isn't necessarily worse than sex with an orgasm.

Orgasm achieved. Sex completed. End of romantic encounter.

2) Don't rush it. People with vaginas typically take longer than people with penises to reach orgasm. That's OK. If your partner is giving you head for 30 minutes they probably love it, and probably really like you too. So stop worrying about their jaw ache and take as long as you need.

3) Talk about it! Don't let it become a taboo subject. If you share your concern with your partner you're less likely to get stressed about it and are therefore more likely to orgasm.

Accept that you might never have an orgasm from soley penetrative sex. AND IT DOESN'T MATTER

"Vaginal" orgasms aren't necessarily better than clitoral ones.

INSECURE FIND YOUR G-SPOT

AND CHANGE YOUR LIFE
YES!

Most orgasms happen from clitoral stimulation, and sticking a penis in a vagina isn't a very efficient way of stimulating the clitoris. So let it go. Ask for more. A vaginal orgasm isn't the holy grail. You're not missing out, or "broken", or letting anyone down if you can't orgasm from penetrative sex.

If you can orgasm from internal stimulation, fab! If not? Fab!

Most women don't orgasm from vaginal penetrative sex on it's own. It's some big ol' myth that this is the "best" or most "powerful" way for women to have an orgasm. For every human body part there is probably a woman out there who can orgasm if you rub her's the right way. All these orgasms will feel different, but none is inherently better than any other.

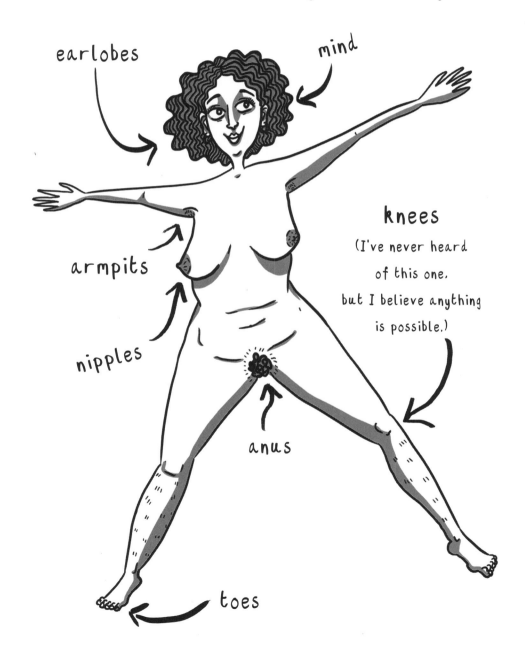

earlobes

mind

knees
(I've never heard
of this one,
but I believe anything
is possible.)

armpits

nipples

anus

toes

No one really knows why some women can orgasm through penetration alone and some can't. But the answer is probably physical, rather than, as Sigmund Freud claimed, a lack of maturity. Or not having tried the right penis yet. Or not being good enough at sex.

Soz, babes, I was bullshitting about the vaginal orgasms.

You're joking! I've been looking for it for years!

Or that you just haven't found your G-spot yet, as many women's magazines spent the 1990s telling us. The G-spot doesn't actually exist - not as a sure physical thing that doctors can identify. Some scientists think that women who can orgasm from vaginal penetration have more-pronounced remnants of a female prostate gland (that's the thing that boys have that means they love putting things up their bum so much*). And this is what the mythical G-spot could actually be.

*Not all boys, of course! But don't knock it 'til you've tried it, fellas.

Men are taught from a young age that sex is all about their pleasure, while women are taught that sex is about pleasing your man and making babies!

Let go of the belief that all sex needs to involve penetration. Instead of trying for ages to have a vaginal orgasm, why not use that energy to do more of the things you know do give you orgasms? People generally like watching their partner orgasm. So you receiving more pleasure will also in turn probably give your partner more pleasure too.

Talking about sex can feel embarrassing and scary. But it's worth it. Telling your partner what you want is 100% the best way to have more orgasms during sex.

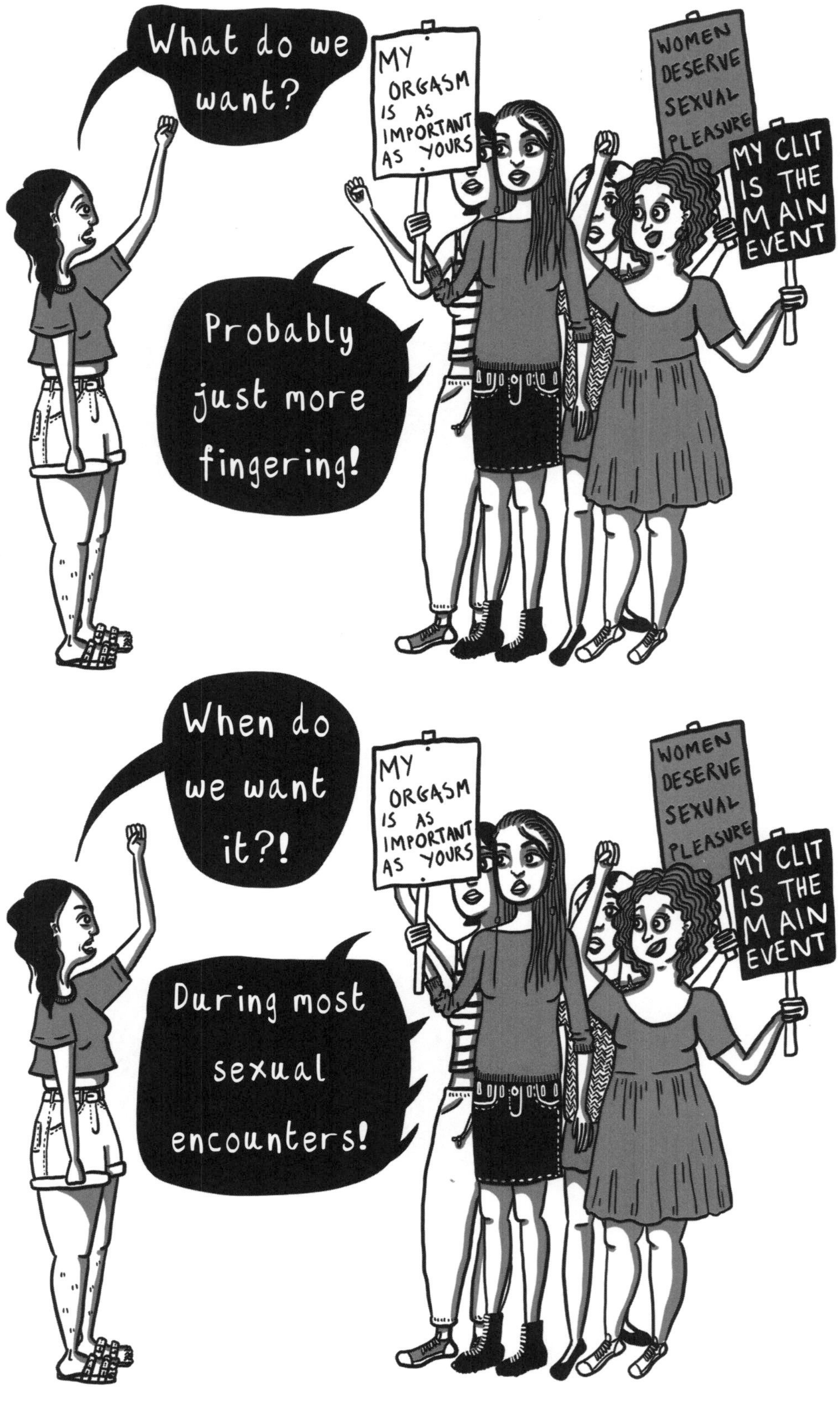
What do we want?
MY ORGASM IS AS IMPORTANT AS YOURS
WOMEN DESERVE SEXUAL PLEASURE
MY CLIT IS THE MAIN EVENT
Probably just more fingering!
When do we want it?!
MY ORGASM IS AS IMPORTANT AS YOURS
WOMEN DESERVE SEXUAL PLEASURE
MY CLIT IS THE MAIN EVENT
During most sexual encounters!

FAKING ORGASMS

Most women have faked an orgasm at some point in their lives. Why do we do it? Because we care so much about other people's feelings? Or because we feel pressure to be able to come during penetrative sex?
Or because it's easier than saying...

If you're having a one-night stand, and you know it's gonna be a one-night stand, there isn't that much harm in faking an orgasm. Maybe it will make their day! Sure, it's lying, and lying is bad, but it's a white lie. I'm not saying you should fake an orgasm. But if you do currently sometimes act all YES OH GOD YES with some guy you met in All Bar One, whose name might be Geoff or Jeremy you're not really sure, it doesn't make you a bad feminist. There are bigger problems in the world. I wouldn't waste energy feeling guilty about it.

However if you LIKE like the person, don't fake an orgasm. It's a bad road to go down. In a relationship you should feel comfortable enough to say, it's not gonna happen for me tonight.

I think I might be too drunk to come.

I'm sorry, I just can't get out of my head tonight.

I really enjoy this type of sex, but I don't come from it.

I'm sorry, I think I masturbated too much this afternoon to come.

You're doing everything right, but it's just not happening for me tonight.

If you want to have better sex, you have to learn to communicate openly about it, and that includes telling them if you are struggling to orgasm.

If you've faked an orgasm with your partner, come clean, apologize and try not to do it again.

SQUIRTING

Squirting, or female ejaculation, is when a woman produced a burst of liquid out of her vulva when she climaxes. There is no reliable data about how many women squirt. Some women squirt a lot. Some women never squirt. Some women squirt once and then never again. All the above is normal.

So what is it, Doctor?

Um, probably not pee.

There also isn't very much science on what squirting actually is. Scientists really disagree on the big question: is it just a lil' bit of pee? The answer is that, for some women, yes, it probably is pee, but also for most women it's probably something else, similar to prostate fluid.

If you make someone squirt, fan-fucking-tastic. Well done you, seriously bask in that pride. Print yourself off a certificate, write it in your diary. Make the 17th of January National "Day I First Made a Lady Squirt" Day in your heart. But, sorry to rain on your parade, it has probably got more to do with the particular arrangement of her anatomy than anything special you did.

Squirting gets some serious over-representation in porn, which can lead men who grew up watching it to think that this should be a goal of sex for all women. Not all women can squirt. In fact, probably not very many of them can at all. And that's OK. If a man really wants to make you squirt, tell him you are happy for him to try as much as he likes, but he shouldn't make himself, or you, feel less-than for not having this fun party trick in your repertoire.

DESIRE

One of the biggest sexual complaints in relationships is a mismatch of sexual desire. One partner wants more sex than the other.

Our level of desire can change throughout our lives, menstrual cycles and relationships. What changes it isn't as simple as hormones, or finding your partner sexy or not. Our sexual desire is linked to the context of our whole lives, and everything in our lives has the potential to make us want more or less sex.

We're used to talking about "sex drive", but it's more complicated than that. Rather than having a big sex drive or a small sex drive, it makes more sense to think of everyone having a sex accelerator and a sex brake.

Some people have a more sensitive accelerator and some people might have a more sensitive brake. Things that turn you on hit your sex accelerator, while things that turn you off hit your sex brake. This is known as the dual-control model of sexual response, and it was developed by Erick Janssen and John Bancroft at the Kinsey institute.

Yes, this theory was developed by two white male sexologists, but it's a useful way of thinking about your sex life and this is still a book about feminism! And yes, you too can be a sexologist when you grow up.

People with sensitive brakes might find it difficult to get aroused unless conditions are just right for them, while people with a sensitive accelerator might find themselves getting aroused more often and sometimes in seemingly random situations.

My Granny is over for dinner, so this would be a really bad time to feel horny, but because of my sensitive accelerator the fact that my partner has made such a nice dinner is turning me on...

Even the fact that you have a sensitive brake can hit your brake. If you've ever found it difficult to come because you think you're taking too long to come, then that's your brake hitting your brake.

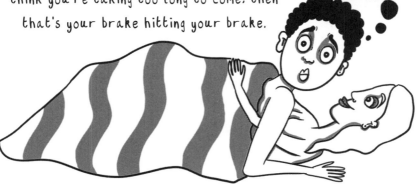

OMG Pete, just ejaculate already!

And things that turn you on and hit your accelerator won't always work if there's too much hitting your brake. For example, if your partner cooks dinner for you and wears really nice underwear and suggests you go to bed early, these might all be things that are likely to turn you on. But if you had a really stressful day at work and can't stop thinking about that annoying email you got, and your partner still hasn't taken the bin out and you're still kind of annoyed at them for it, all the nice things they've done might not be enough to overrule all that sexual braking.

Everyone has a different level of sensitivity when it comes to sex brakes and accelerators.

I have a sensitive brake and an average accelerator. In the right context I don't find it difficult to get aroused. But I'm very sensitive to all the reasons not to be turned on.

I have a not so sensitive accelerator and a sensitive brake. I need a lot of stimuli to become turned on, and if something's not right I can be easily turned off.

I have a sensitive accelerator and a not so sensitive brake. I respond easily to erotic stimuli, even smell and taste. And I sometimes become aroused in awkward situations.

I have an average brake but a not so sensitive accelerator. I find it difficult to become aroused and need a lot of cues to get going. But once I am aroused it's great!

Learning what hits your accelerator

How can we make ourselves want more sex? You can't just take a pill, despite what Sex In The City told you about female viagra. You can't change how sensitive your brake or accelerator is. You have to examine what's turning you on and increase its presence in your life. And find out what's turning you off and find ways to minimize it in your life.

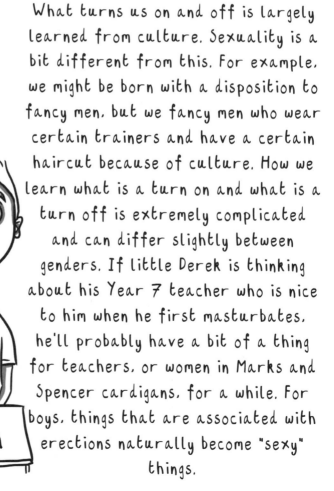

What turns us on and off is largely learned from culture. Sexuality is a bit different from this. For example, we might be born with a disposition to fancy men, but we fancy men who wear certain trainers and have a certain haircut because of culture. How we learn what is a turn on and what is a turn off is extremely complicated and can differ slightly between genders. If little Derek is thinking about his Year 7 teacher who is nice to him when he first masturbates, he'll probably have a bit of a thing for teachers, or women in Marks and Spencer cardigans, for a while. For boys, things that are associated with erections naturally become "sexy" things.

Girls don't have a big thing between their legs that obviously lets them know when something is sexy. Because of this, women (or people born with vaginas) often learn what's sexy in more of a social context, i.e. they are more influenced by what other people find sexy.

Both sexes learn what to think of as sexy in a social and a more solo way. The important thing to remember is that what turns us on isn't innate, it's learned and therefore flexible and ever evolving.

What turns you on doesn't have to be just romantic candle-lit dinners and men wearing a bow tie without a shirt (actually, does anyone find this particularly attractive?).

It can be the smell of your partner when they come back from the gym.

Well hello there...

The act of service when your partner changes the bed sheets.

The fear of doing it somewhere where you might get caught.

TESBURY'S

BUY ONE GET ONE FREE

OPEN

FRE

Don't worry, Colin, the cheese aisle is very private.

Your partner opening up emotionally to you.

I have a phobia of baked beans.

I totally get it, babe.

And then Sheila was all like...

Your partner telling a funny anecdote from work.

Your sexuality is complex, and in all likelihood it's not just traditionally sexy things that turn you on.

Try to remember a really good sexual encounter you had

List things that you remember happening before and during it:

_____

_____

_____

_____

_____

_____

_____

_____

_____

_____

_____

_____

_____

_____

Some of the things you listed are hopefully things that really turn you on. If you want to have more sex you can try to increase the presence of these things in your life.

Learning what hits your brake

Finding out why we don't want sex sometimes is more complicated than being aware of what is making us want sex - mainly because in our modern lives there are SO MANY REASONS NOT TO WANT SEX. Our lives are incredibly stressful. Fitting in sex can be HARD. But, if we want to fit it in, first we have to notice what's getting in the way. Here are some of of the many things that can put women off sex:

Negative body image

As we said before, being concerned about what you look like, or not believing that your partner finds you physically attractive, can be a major turn off.

If I leave with him now, everyone will know...

Worrying about what other people will think of you

Worrying that if you have sex with someone everyone else will think you're a slut, or worrying that the person you're having sex with will think you're bad in bed, is a turn off.

Unwanted pregnancy or sexually transmitted diseases

The fear of getting knocked up when it's not the right time for you, or catching an STD, is a major turn off; especially if your partner doesn't seem concerned about taking precautions.

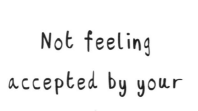

Feeling used by your partner

Many women quite enjoy feeling objectified, but, for some, feeling like a living blow-up doll can be a major turn off.

Not feeling accepted by your partner

If your partner asks you to change too much about yourself, or the way you look or act during sex, it can hit the brakes hard.

The build up

If someone comes on to you too quickly it can shut down your interest in having sex with them.

External reasons

You're worried someone might catch you. His sheets smell bad. You can hear your three-year-old watching Peppa Pig in the next room. The list is endless.

Being in a bad mood

This is probably the most common one of all. Whether it's external stress in other areas of your life, or you're just a bit pissed off with your partner, it's probably the hardest one to overcome.

There are probably even more reasons you can think of why you might not want to have sex. Really, it's a miracle anyone has sex at all.

THE HONEYMOON PERIOD

Then

Now

Why do we often overcome all these turn offs so easily in the first part of a relationship? During the early part of any relationship the bond is insecure; we're not sure if the other person is that into us. So the deep, unconscious, caveman-like part of our brain wants to have sex with our partner all the time, because each time we have sex we are, in theory, strengthening that bond and getting them to stick around a little bit longer. And it feels fantastic!

Later on in our relationships we are hopefully pretty sure our partner likes us. They've seen us puke everywhere after that time we swallowed too much sea water (god it was horrible), and we've done some lethal farts in front of them. So once they've seen us do all that and are still sticking around, we're pretty sure they like us. We don't feel the need to have sex with them to strengthen the bond so much. Kind of sucks, huh?

If you've ever had a massive row with your partner and had amazing sex afterwards, this is the same thing. The massive row ruptures your bond, and when you've made up a bit your body wants to have sex to strengthen that bond again.

YOU DON'T HAVE TO WANT MORE SEX

If you follow our media it can feel as though not having sex three times a week means your relationship isn't perfect. And if you're having sex less than once a week you're heading for a divorce.

FEEL Worse £2.99

How To Please Your Man MORE!

GIVE THE BEST HEAD EVER

How Much Sex SHOULD you be having?

After I gave birth to Lulu we didn't have sex for two months! Can you believe?

If you're only having sex once a year or never at all and you and your partner are happy with that, that's fine. You can still have a great relationship where you are each other's emotional support and provide other physical affection towards each other.

♥ 12,073
Being Intimate with your life partner is so important. I try to have sexual relations with David at least once a week to keep our relationship strong for our kids.

#mom #mommy #we #love #life

However, it's rare for two people in a relationship to be equally happy about not having sex any more. Sexual compatibility is important in a relationship. There will always be compromise, but if one of you wants it three times a week, and the other one three times a year, something's gonna give.

BUT WHAT IF YOU DO WANT MORE SEX?

How do you fix all this? How do you turn the offs off? And the ons on? And re-create that urge to bond that you felt in the honeymoon period, without having a massive row every time? Well, you can't.

It won't ever feel as easy as it did in the honeymoon period. You have to work together by talking and thinking about it and putting in effort. It isn't simple and you'll always be working on it. #love amirite?

Yeah, it's tough. This might mean date nights. It might mean being more open and talking about your feelings more, to help strengthen that urge to bond. It might mean some kinky sex games.

Some problems are easier to fix than others. You could ask Grandma to have the kids for a night so you don't hear Peppa Pig through the walls on a Saturday morning.

But then suddenly Grandma has agreed it's the only opportunity you've had to have a romantic evening in 18 months and the pressure becomes too much and your body shuts down, and all you want to do is sleep.

Not everything will work, and even the stuff that does work won't work every time. And that's OK.

TRUSTING YOUR BRAIN OVER YOUR BODY

Just because you're wet doesn't mean you want it and vice versa

Some clever scientists have done lots of studies on this life-changing thing called "genital non-concordance". Basically, they put a thing around a man's willy to measure his erection, put a tray over his lap so he can't see his willy, and give him a dial to report how turned on he feels, and then show him a load of videos. All types of porn, and a couple of non-sexy videos too. What they found was that there was about a 50% overlap between what men said turned them on and what made them get an erection. That might not sound like that much, but it's a significant correlation. Generally, men's genital response matched to their sexuality and what they reported they felt turned on by.

human man

"how turned on are you" dial

various types of porn

erection-measuring machine.
(I have no idea what these look like)

The same clever scientists did a similar study with women. They put a thing in their vagina to measure blood flow (increased blood flow to the genitals is a thing that typically happens during arousal), showed them a load of videos and got them to report how horny they were. The overlap between women saying they felt turned on and when there was increased blood flow to their genitals was just 10%. Basically there is virtually no correlation between a woman saying she feels horny and her genitals physically responding.

Men

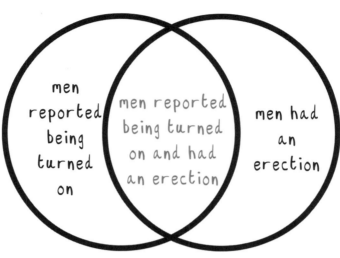

men reported being turned on

men reported being turned on and had an erection

men had an erection

women reported being turned on and had physical signs of arousal

Women

women reported being turned on

women had physical signs of arousal

Another clever scientist did a similar study, but as well as showing women porn, and boring videos of how to fix your dishwasher, they also showed them videos of animals, specifically bonobo apes, having sex. What they found was that women were just as likely to get an increased blood flow to their vagina while watching bonobo apes have sex as they were when looking at humans.

What does all this mean? Do all women secretly want to have sex with a monkey? No. Of course not. I can personally vouch that I definitely don't want to have sex with a monkey.

Well, thanks a lot. Not that interested in you either actually, Flo.

What it probably means is that your vagina responds to most sexually relevant things, whether you want to get involved with them or not. But just because something makes you wet doesn't mean you are turned on, or that you want to get involved with it.

Oh, thank god.

It also means your vagina is an unreliable diva who gets wet when she feels like it and not necessarily when you want her to. So if you want to have sex but you're partner says, "But you're not wet?!" simply explain sexual non-concordance to them and then go grab some lube. Bless lube.

And if you ever don't want sex but are wet, that means nothing. Trust your gut, your heart, and your head over whatever your vagina is up to. Your vagina is just responding to sexually relevant things; your head decides if you want that thing or not. And anyone who trusts your vagina over your head is trash.

These results aren't new, and the monkey study rightly got a lot of media attention, mainly because it's funny that apes make girls wet lololol. So why doesn't everyone already know about non-concordance?

Is it perhaps the patriarchy, Flo?

Why yes, however did you know?

Because men have a greater genital response to feeling turned on, we assume that that must be the norm. That is crap. Men and women are different in this case. And women's version isn't less than or broken. Also this happens to men too! Most men have wanted to have sex and not been able to get it up. Hello, non-concordance. And a lot of men wake up with a slightly inconvenient erection most mornings (Yeah, you again, non-concordance, we get it.)

Our bodies aren't perfectly working machines that always act and react conveniently. Listen to your gut and your brain. And use lube - it's amazing! (No, I'm not sponsored by lube, but I wish I was.)

PLAY LUBE

Glide
So wet and slippy

Little bit on orgasm non-concordance

For some women, not all orgasms are pleasurable; sometimes they are damn right inconvenient. We are complex creatures, and sometimes they happen when we're not expecting them or wanting them. People can orgasm during sexual assault. Just because someone had an orgasm doesn't necessarily mean they enjoyed or wanted the sex.

Basically, trust what comes out of someone's mouth, not what their body does.

Women can also have orgasms during childbirth, medical procedures, exercise and long journeys on old diesel buses. Amirite, ladies?

STRESS AND SEX

When we're stressed, things that we would have found erotic before now probably only make us more stressed. What we find pleasurable in one scenario, we won't find pleasurable in every scenario or emotional state.

How our bodies respond to stress hasn't changed since the days when our main source of stress was being chased by lions. We evolved so stress would pump us full of horrible hormones that make us want to run away from lions or lie on the ground very still and play dead.

There are only two outcomes to being chased by a lion. Either you die, in which case, oh well. Or you survive and you feel amazing. Modern problems aren't like that. But when we think about that credit-card bill we're still gonna feel like we're about to be chased by a lion.

When it comes to feelings, it helps me to think of them as real physical things, which they are! There is a complex cocktail of hormones and electrical currents buzzing about your brain making you feel the way you feel at any given moment. They affect you the same way drugs affect you. You can't ignore feelings. If you are drunk you can't just say "I'm not drunk" and then drive. Just like if you're sad, you can't simply declare "I'm not sad" and be horny. You have to eat a big kebab and wait eight hours before you can drive after drinking. To get over feelings, you have to acknowledge them and find a way to get through them.

You have to work out what you can do to safely feel your feelings and get to the other side. You need to acknowledge the behaviours that you use to distract yourself and push these feelings down. And avoid overindulging in them.

Just one more episode.

Find the behaviours that you use to get through to the other side of your feelings.

running

having a long bath

dancing

AHH-HHH-HHH-HHH

having a big scream

And you'll never guess what she said next.

bitchin'

MY FEELINGS
· Bad
· Sad
· Mad
· Sanitary Pad.

writing a list

crying

ZZzz

sleeping

Avoid any behaviours that could hurt you or others around you. If you really don't know what behaviours help you, there are two which work for almost everyone: exercise, and talking about it out loud. We have evolved to get happy hormones from running around and making relationships, and my god are those happy hormones nice. But sometimes you can't make yourself feel better instantly, and it will need a lot more work. That might mean lifestyle changes, time, or therapy. Working on yourself and improving your average mood is one of the most important and rewarding things you can possibly do. And every time you take a step in that direction you should be incredibly proud of yourself.

I bought a book about sex and I thought it would be really jokes, and then it told me to consider therapy if I wanted to improve my sex life!

Oh, that sounds terrible. I'm so sorry.

Think back to a time in the past when you were really stressed or sad. What made you feel better? What gave you that feeling of release from those feelings? And what behaviours didn't move you on?

Helpful behaviours: Unhelpful behaviours:

_____   _____

_____   _____

_____   _____

_____   _____

_____   _____

_____   _____

_____   _____

_____   _____

_____   _____

_____   _____

_____   _____

_____   _____

Next time you're going through some stuff you can look back on this list to help you get through your feelings.

CONSENT

- it's the hot topic to shout at your weird uncle about after one too many brandies on Boxing Day.

I just think it's a witch-hunt out there for men today.

The #MeToo movement has catapulted consent into public awareness. And I'm so glad about that. Consent is brilliant. Consent should be involved in every sexual experience you have. But it's not as simple as it's often painted to be. Consent isn't often about saying "yes" or "no". Humans, especially British and other repressed humans, are so bad at saying what they actually mean. For example, if you're in the pub and someone says, "One more drink, Jim?" we don't usually just say, "No thanks, Colin." We will more naturally say something like:

Got to get back to the missus you know, and I need to hit the gym tomorrow. This sexy bod needs some maintenance.

Or, "I'm trying to cut down," or, "I'm a bit tired, mate." We give excuses. In our culture it's seen as rude to just say "no".

Consent is often denied in subtle ways, covered in excuses and body language. I'm not saying this is how it should be. Ideally, humans would just say what they actually mean all the time. But we don't.

I'm not saying that all of these examples are ways of saying "no"; sometimes, someone might feel unsure but then decide "yes".

We should encourage men to actively check for consent. Usually, people do give obvious verbal and non-verbal cues that they want to have sex, like asking about condoms. But if someone isn't doing that, if you feel that someone is unsure, or if you feel like you are leading the sexual encounter completely, maybe just check. There is nothing hotter than someone asking, "Can I fuck you?" And someone else saying, "Yes, please, I would like that very much."

We have to stop playing along with the narrative that men are entitled to sex, that just because a man is a "nice guy", or because he takes a girl out on an extravagant date, or because it's Valentine's Day and he took his girlfriend to Paris, he somehow deserves sex. Men are only entitled to sex when someone else wants to have sex with them, and for no other reason.

Perhaps what we should do is actually encourage our children to say "no". And listen to and respect them when they do. Obviously, if they are saying "no" to eating any vegetables you're gonna have to call rank with them on that one. But if they don't wanna hug creepy Aunty Meredith, who they've only just met, then maybe don't make them. Women are socialized from such an early age to prioritize pleasing others over their own feelings. If we stop doing that, then more women are going to be empowered throughout their life to take themselves away from situations they aren't enjoying.

The line between bad sex and sexual assault isn't completely black and white. Humans are far too complicated for that. The same thing can happen to two different people and one might call it sexual assault, and the other might call it bad sex. The problem comes when the person who would call it just bad sex denies the person who calls it sexual assault the right to call it that. They are failing to empathize with the other person's terrible experience and denying the other person's experience of their pain.

"Believe all women" doesn't mean "Proscecute all men". There are different standards of proof in the law and in real life, and rightly so. Not every person who sexually assaults someone should be legally punished. It's depressing, but sexual assault can be impossible to prove, and you need solid proof when you're dealing with the law. But every person who has been sexually assaulted should be believed and supported. If you feel like you've been sexually assaulted, then you have, even if the law doesn't agree, or other people have a different definition for what you went through. Your pain is still real.

I got my phone nicked in a club. I was really upset, but I didn't report it to the police because I didn't have the time and the club has no CCTV anyway. It would be hard to prove I didn't just lose my phone.

My manager flashed me at work. I reported him to HR and got him fired. They asked me if I wanted to file a police report and I declined. I felt like he'd been punished enough and I didn't want to think about it any more.

The best we can do is educate everyone on what consent is and how to get it. Consent is about human communication, which is messy and unreliable. We are always going to disagree sometimes. We have to keep talking about it, and normalize more communication before and during sex.

HOW TO BE A KINKY FEMINIST

Kinky stuff isn't for everyone. If you have no interest from straying from your vanilla lifestyle, feel free to skip this chapter. (Of course you won't skip this chapter; you wanna know what all the kinky people are up to you nosey lil' vanilla cupcake.)

You got me!

But what if you are having fantasies that involve more than just having sex in a bed with the person you're already having sex with? First of all, just because you're fantasizing about it doesn't mean you have to actually do it.

That was amazing Theresa. And Boris, I never would have guessed!

Oh, thank god!

Fantasies are really fun. You can do whatever you like! Wanna have sex with some squidman or your boyfriend's dad? Go for it, as long as it's in your brain. Because squidmen don't exist (as far as I know??? Sorry if you're a squidperson reading this), and having sex with your boyfriend's dad would probably really fuck up your life and not be worth it (probably, though you never know, right??).

Just because you fantasize about something doesn't even mean you would want to do it in real life. In your head you might like the idea of having sex with four strangers in an alleyway, but if you actually got into that situation you might feel afraid, or cold and uncomfortable. Because you're in an alleyway.

As long as something's just in your head, there's no point in feeling guilty about it - you don't have to go through with it in real life. But what if you do want to do it? You've thought about it, and you wanna try a threesome/sex outside/putting something up your bum/getting spanked. What next?

Find someone you trust. Every time we get naked with another person we are making ourselves vulnerable in an exciting and beautiful way. This is even more true when we get kinky with someone else, so you might want to be extra careful that you are sure that the person you're getting kinky with knows it is all a game. Maybe don't try getting blindfolded for the first time with a guy you just met in Spoons.

Being kinky usually means playing around with a power dynamic (submissive or dominant). Both roles can make you quite vulnerable. So the first and most important piece of advice is: you have to find the right person. If you want to try something different in bed, you need someone who you can trust to stop when you say "stop" (or "mackerel", "tiddlywinks", or whatever else you decide your safeword is). Once you've found someone you wanna get kinky with you should talk in detail about your fantasies.

Ideally, sex should be like going to dinner at someone's house. You invite someone for dinner, ask if they're a vegetarian, cook them something you both like to eat, and if they refuse pudding it's not a big deal, you'll have it for breakfast. Imagine if we asked as much detail about someone's preferences before sex as we do the first time we cook them dinner.

Don't try everything at once. Don't put your biggest dildo in that hole unless you've had a finger in there first and liked it. Before you move on and try anything new, check that you're both still into it. Consent at every level.

CONSENT CAN BE HOT

It's basically just dirty talk. But some people find dirty talk excruciating. So how do you get over your embarrassment around talking about sex?

Start by talking about sex more with your mates.

What's the kinkiest thing you've ever done?

Remember the weird shed behind college...

What are your general thoughts about sex toys?

Curious?

Move on to talking about sex with your partner in a more abstract way.

You could watch some porn together as a conversation prompt, talk about what you like and don't like about what you see.

I don't like how she's done her hair.

Dear Boyfriend,
I wanna use a butt plug.
Love,
your girlfriend!
xoxo

If you really can't bear to talk about sex with your partner face to face, write them a sexy letter.

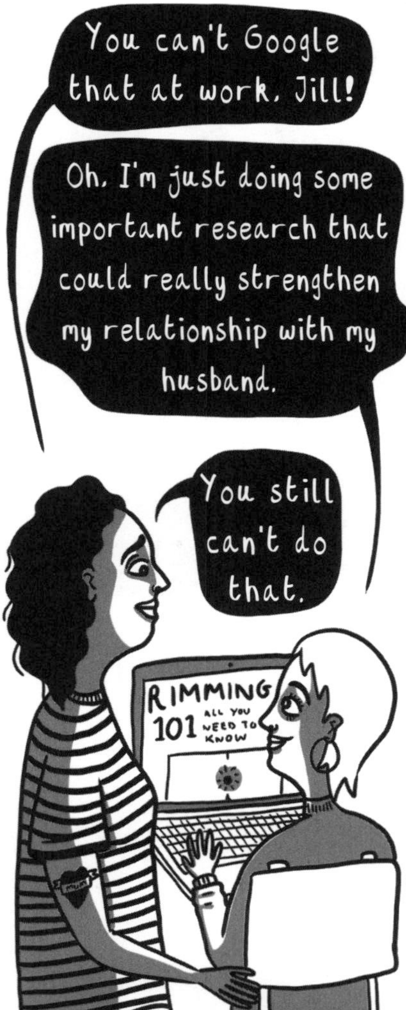
You can't Google that at work, Jill!
Oh, I'm just doing some important research that could really strengthen my relationship with my husband.
You still can't do that.
RIMMING 101 ALL YOU NEED TO KNOW

What should you do if your partner asks you to do something in bed that isn't something you've fantasized about before? Try not to kink-shame them - be open-minded. Ask them to give you some time to think about it. Imagine yourself in that scenario: does it turn you on? Watch porn of that kink - horny yet? If you enjoy thinking about it, and enjoy watching the porn, give it a go. If you're not into it, communicate that, and hopefully it won't be a deal breaker for your sexual compatibility. Don't do something you don't want to just to please your partner. But, it doesn't have to be a big deal to try something once. And by indulging your partner's fantasy you might learn something about yourself.

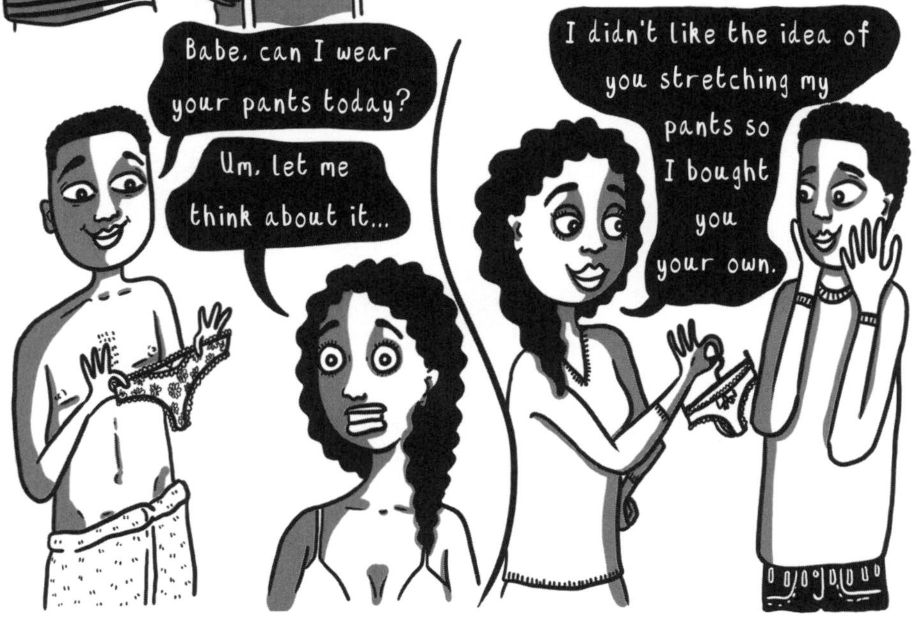
Babe, can I wear your pants today?
Um, let me think about it...
I didn't like the idea of you stretching my pants so I bought you your own.

Often, the things that seem most taboo to us are the things that turn us on most. It's why CEOs tend to like being stood on by women in stilettos.

And some of the most feminist women like being called a dirty slut.

If you're not feeling it, say so. It's never too late to back out. Even if you're already all tied up, you've bought the spanking paddle, and lit the candles, it's not too late. If your partner tries to persuade you to do something you're not comfortable with that isn't cool. That's trash.

Just because someone wants something once, doesn't mean they'll want to do it every time they have sex. Make sure you and your partner check for consent every time you try anything. Trust me, it makes it sexier.

HAVING SEX ON YOUR PERIOD

No woman should be made to feel gross or "unclean" on her period. Nor should she feel bad for wanting to have sex on her period. Many women find they want more sex on their period, and many say that orgasms relieve menstrual cramps. There is no denying that period sex can be messy, and if someone isn't into that, that's OK. If you try it on with some and they say...

Soz, babes, not really into period sex.

Then no big deal. However, if they say this ➡ then that's not cool.

EWWWW, NOOOO, THAT'S DISGUSTING

Period sex is perfectly safe and clean, and there are a lot of ways to deal with the mess.

Move over, I'm freezing.

Shower sex! Or a strategically placed towel!

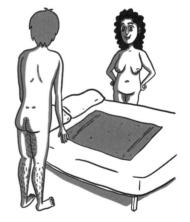

It's incredible the things you can achieve with a tampon in and some lube. The world is your mooncup!

MONOGAMY

Marriage with "the one" is what we're all taught to aspire to. And the vast majority of us do! We spend hours dreaming of our Prince or Princess Charming who's going to commit to spending the rest of their lives with us. A person to raise children with or at least prevent us from dying alone. But not many of us actually end up getting this. 42% of marriages end in divorce.* And for the lucky 58%, half of those people end up dying alone anyway.

HA! I beat you to it, Ethel.

If you were going to have surgery with only a 58% success rate, you'd be feeling pretty shitty. But no one expects to get divorced. Most of us still believe that finding "the one" is the key to our happiness, even with these pretty dismal success rates. Why? Because it's in our human nature to mate for life? Us and penguins are beautiful monogamous creatures designed to mate for life, right??

Actually, we only stick together for one mating season... but sure!

*From the Office of National Statistics in England and Wales. 2013.

Well, probably not. Humans have been rocking around the planet in roughly our current form for about 300,000 years. And a lot of evidence suggests that for the vast majority of that time we've been shagging all over the shop. Bear with me while I bombard you with some evidence that suggests that Mr and Mrs Grunt, who lived three caves down on the right, were most definitely swingers.

Before we started farming (about 10,000 years ago) we lived in hunter-gatherer societies, roaming vast areas collecting whatever food we managed to kill or stumble upon. Much like our cousins the chimps and bonobos. All the evidence we have (from studying modern hunter-gatherer societies as well as reading accounts from the first Europeans who went round the world ruining everything and bumping into these various societies) suggests that they shared absolutely everything, including sexual partners. The idea of individual property only seems to have started once people had farms to defend. Until then, the most important thing was the wellbeing of the group rather than the wellbeing of the individual or of their blood relations.

There is also physical evidence in your body right now that we are evolved to shag multiple people. Firstly, it's important to know just how much like monkeys we are. Chimps and bonobos are more closely related to us than they are to gorillas or orangutans.

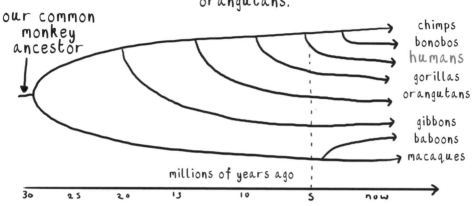

our common
monkey
ancestor

chimps
bonobos
humans
gorillas
orangutans
gibbons
baboons
macaques

millions of years ago

30   25   20   15   10   5   now

Chimps live in social groups with multiple males and females. There tends to be a dominant male who gets first pick of the ladies, but generally everyone ends up shagging everyone else. Bonobos, meanwhile, live in extremely peaceful societies where older females are the highest-ranking members, and man do they bone a lot. Bonobos have sex to say hi, to resolve conflicts, to celebrate eating some nice ants. Basically, bonobos shag like the British talk about the weather. They do it to bond socially; they also masturbate and have oral sex and plenty of homosexual action. Bonobos live a less MDMA-fuelled version of the Channel 4 drama Skins - constantly.

Our more distant relations the gorillas live in groups with one dominant male who does all the sex with his harem of female gorillas. The only apes who live in monogamous relationships are our even more distant relations, the gibbons, who live in small family units.

Unlike humans, we're actually good at monogamy!

By looking at the physical differences between us and our evolutionary cousins we can get an idea of the kind of sexual relationships we evolved to have. Let's start with the contents of everyone's favourite skin sack: testicles! Chimps and bonobos have bloody huge balls. They hang outside the body so they constantly have a load of ready-to-spunk junk on standby. Gorillas, on the other hand, have tiny lil' balls all safely tucked up inside them. Gorillas don't spend much time having sex: they don't mate to socially bond, only to have babies, so they don't need a load of spunk on tap to take advantage of whatever lucky lady they bump into. As anyone who has testicles, has been intimate with testicles, or has drunk in the same bar as a university rugby team, knows, humans have medium-sized balls that hang outside the body.

chimp / bonobo balls
≃ 160g

human balls
≃ 50g

≃ 30g
lil' gorilla balls that don't even look like this because they're all up inside

We have a modest amount of spunk, ready to go at any moment it's required. We've evolved to shag a lot, not just when it's absolutely necessary to make babies. We have this incredibly vulnerable, sensitive, survival nightmare hanging between our legs purely so we can store more sperm.

Gorillas and gibbons have sex less than 20 times in their entire lives. While we, chimps and bonobos have sex on average well over 1,000 times per lifetime. Lucky us, huh?

The next thing to note is the male-female body size dimorphism in humans.

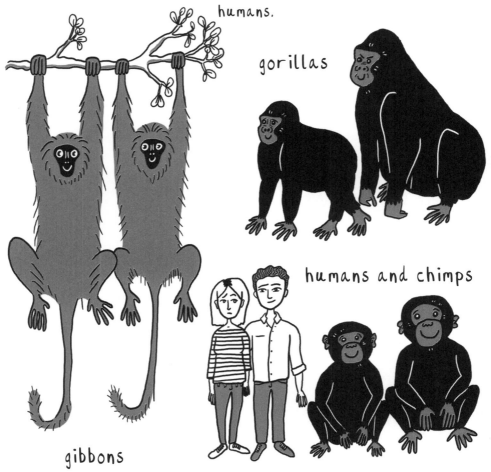

gorillas

humans and chimps

gibbons

Monogamous gibbons have no average size difference between males and females. Why would they need one? Male gibbons don't need to fight other man gibbons for sex, since they've all neatly got their own lady gibbon life partner. Male gorillas, on the other hand, are twice as big as female gorillas. They need to be big and strong to defend their harem from a challenging male. There's a lot of competition in the gorilla world to get in on the action, because it doesn't happen very often. Chimps, bonobos and us have about a 15-20% average size difference between men and women. Basically, there is some competition between human males for sex - more than your faithful gibbon, but a lot less than your harem-style social-group gorilla.

To a lot of Western people today, the idea of a non-monogamous relationship or society is terrifying. There are two big concerns that hit you in the face straight away: jealousy and paternity certainty. Let's start with the paternity certainty argument: how does a dude know that his kid is his kid if his wife has been shagging about? Well, this is what a Jesuit asked when he lived with the Naskapi tribe in what is now Canada.

Both of these are paraphrased, one by me, one by an olden-days Jesuit.

How d'you know your kid is yours, mate?

Thou hast no sense, you French people love only your own children, but we all love all the children of our tribe.

Not entirely sure what either of these two people should be wearing. They were probably both cold, though.

Basically, when the group is more important than your sense of yourself as an individual, who cares whose kids are whose? You're probably all cousins anyway.

How would our hunter-gatherer ancestors even have known that one jizz leads to one baby? They weren't really prioritizing scientific discovery of that kind back then. More preoccupied with the great which-plants-taste-good-which-plants-kill-you-and-which-ones-make-you-high survey of 100,000 BC.

Survey is going great, dude.

When Anthropologists Stephen Beckerman and Paul Valentine spent some time with various tribes of the Amazon, they found a common shared belief in most of the tribes that all sexually active women are a little bit pregnant, and that a baby is formed over time from all the semen of all the men that a woman has had sex with.

Daddies! Meet your baby!

(This theory would really help the plot of the popular musical Mamma Mia!)

What about jealousy, then? Didn't these Amazonian men feel a bit miffed when their hammock buddy was off getting busy with some other dude? Maybe they did, I have no idea. Jealousy obviously exists, but that doesn't mean it's innate to human nature. Fear is innate, but the fear that he's going to leave you for his secretary isn't innate. In the marriage ceremony traditional to the Brazilian tribe of Canela they first vow to stay together until their last child has grown up and then vow not to be too jealous of each other's lovers. That's some proper commitment.

I promise to be cool with it when you're off getting a blow job with Maureen from the next village.

And I promise to always do the dishes if you do the cooking.

Also, would you feel so jealous if you were also getting action somewhere else? Among the Siriono of Bolivia, jealousy happens not when your spouse has lovers, but when they are devoting too much time to these lovers. Sex is thought of as a hunger that needs to be satisfied, separate from love.

Allan Holmberg, who lived with the Siriono, noted that they "rarely, if ever, lack for sexual partners". When no one is monogamous, there's always someone around to have a quickie with.

Which of you dudes is up for it, because my Jackie Collins novel has got a bit hot and heavy and I'm gonna need a shag before I can focus on the plot again.

We know that the honeymoon period can't last for ever. Lust fades - you don't rip your clothes off with excitement the 1,000th time you sleep with someone. Jealousy is a negative emotion, but so is wanting to bang someone new and not being able to. Why do we say that jealousy is a reasonable emotion that is grounds for divorce, but wanting to bang someone new is a dirty feeling that should be suppressed? Men and women have risked their families, financial security, jobs and even lives all because they realllyyyyy wanted to shag someone else. Adultery is punishable by stoning to death in Iran, but people still do it! Doesn't seem like an emotion that is that easy to ignore to me.

I'm not saying that everyone should be polyamorous. I've never been in a polyamorous relationship, so I have no idea what it's like.

Actually, imaginary boyfriend, I take it all back: monogamy for ever!!

And I'm not saying that just because humans haven't evolved to be monogamous means we're all incapable of it. We do lots of things we're not evolved to do. Like living in lovely centrally heated flats and sleeping on memory-foam mattresses. Also, life is obviously very different from what it was when we all lived in the jungle. In hunter-gatherer societies there was no fear of growing old alone. You are constantly surrounded by your tribe, so who cares if you have a nuclear family unit? You're surrounded by the only people you've ever known 24/7. You and your neighbour Colin share all the same interests because the only thing there is to be interested in is jungle stuff. You probably wouldn't know what it is like to be lonely if you've grown up in the same close-knit community of 100 or so people your whole life. On the other hand, they had to eat bugs, and probably did some casual killing of the extra babies. So it wasn't all rosy!

Wanna bone, Colin?

Yeah, sure, just let me finish my worm sandwich.

You don't have to do something just because the society you grow up in expects it of you. You don't have to get married to avoid dying old alone. Value your non-romantic relationships as much as your romantic ones. For pretty much all of human history, marriage has been a way of controlling women, a way for fathers to sell off their daughters to another man who provides for her in exchange for sex and babies. But now that women can own property and be financially independent (yay!), we don't need to get married if we don't want to.

Monogamy should be a choice, just like waxing your pubes off, becoming vegetarian or putting stuff up your bum. Humans are all so complicated and different. Monogamy isn't easy, but neither is any other option; having relationships with other humans is always going to be complicated and difficult.

What makes one human happy on Monday might not make even that same human happy on Wednesday. Nor is there one formula for a happy life, or good sex, that fits with every human the world over. I'm not telling you to definitely try having a non-monogamous relationship. I'm just suggesting that the narratives we've all been sold our whole lives might not be the right fit for you.

PORN

Porn isn't new. Ever since humans have been creating images they've been creating images of naked people getting it on.

Really some of your best work, Carol. Brings the cave to life.

What is new is how widely available porn is and how unrealistic it is. Watching porn can be really fun. It's hot. Don't worry, I'm not gonna tell anyone to stop watching porn. But porn isn't sex education. In fact, it's the precise opposite. The vast majority of porn looks nothing like the sex that most people have. And the vast majority of women don't look like the average woman you see in porn. And although the science is still very new, studies are starting to show that porn is addictive.

You wanna come back to mine or...

Actually, I have a way more reliable orgasm if I just masturbate to Cheerleader Orgy 3. I had a lovely time, though!

If you're a young gal who knows the ways of the world, you've probably had the experience where a man contorts you into a position that you're pretty sure isn't that pleasurable for either of you, just because it provides a good angle for an imaginary camera. And it's shit.

Yasss, Carol, you look fantastic!

Hurry up, I can't hold this for long!

There is also evidence that porn has vastly increased erectile dysfunction in men. It seems there's a bit of an epidemic that men in their teens and twenties have watched so much porn they can't get it up for real-life ladies. Which is just depressing.

Just give me one second...

Actually, you're alright.

Porn doesn't show people having conversations about consent or women who can't be arsed to shave their legs. It shows women gagging on cocks, and being pounded for ages extremely hard. And, worst of all, lesbians having sex with fake nails. And unless you literally type in PUBES I WOULD LIKE TO SEE PUBES PLEASE PORNHUB, you will not see a single stray hair.

I'm not sure teenagers are grasping how unrealistic this is. I don't know what's happening inside teenagers' brains - as a childless 26-year-old woman I rarely spend time with them. But if you happen to know a teenager just grab it and tell it that porn is about as realistic for sex as 'Game Of Thrones' is for twin sibling relations.

If you enjoy watching porn, good for you, carry on. But be aware that porn is just porn, it's not what real sex should look like. if you're comparing yourself to porn, stop that nonsense immediately. Real sex is better than porn. Real naked ladies are better than in-your-phone naked ladies. And lesbians with fake nails is just damn right dangerous.

NUDES

You can't give humanity smartphones and expect them not to constantly send naked photos to each other. COME ON. It would be like giving my cat opposable thumbs and telling him he's still not allowed to open his own packets of vacuum-packed meat. My cat loves vacuum-packed meat, and humans love looking at each others genitals.

OH COME ON!

But sadly we don't live in a sexual utopia. And maybe you, quite understandably, don't want everyone you know to see you naked. So should you send a nude?

Pssst, most people are nice and won't post your nudes online.

First question. Do you want to send a nude? Does the idea of the recipient of the nude (let's call them the Nudee) getting horny to a picture of you naked make you excited? If no, then probably don't send the nude.

If everyone you work with saw the nude, would you be fired? The liklihood of this happening is very, very low. So the question isn't, "Do you want everyone you work with to see the nude?" because obviously, for most people, we don't want all our colleagues to see us naked. But if your nude somehow went viral (don't flatter yourself, you ain't that special, it probably won't happen), would you get fired? The only people I can really think of that should be really, really careful about sending nudes are: A-list celebrities, politicians, and most of all teachers. If I was a teacher I wouldn't send a nude. You just don't want a class of 16-year-olds to get hold of a naked photo of you.

Does the idea of your nudee showing all their mates this nude freak you out? If yes, probably don't send the nude. The thing is, human beings are kind creatures; we love to share. And a lot of people will show their mates the nudes they've received. This can mean anything from a quick flash of their phone screen - "OMG, look how hot this dick pic I just got sent is!" - to dropping it in a WhatsApp group which accidentally has your ex in it which your nudee forgot about. How much do you care? And how much do you trust your nudee?

Are you under 16? Then for god's sake don't send a nude - that's child porn and everyone involved can get in serious shit. But if you're an adult who wants to send a nude, who has a willing nudee, who has a regular job where no one cares what they get up to in the bedroom, go for it! It's not that big a deal. And if you're really worried just crop your face out.

Only take hot nudes!

Because, god forbid they do get in the wrong hands, you at least want them to be something you're proud of.

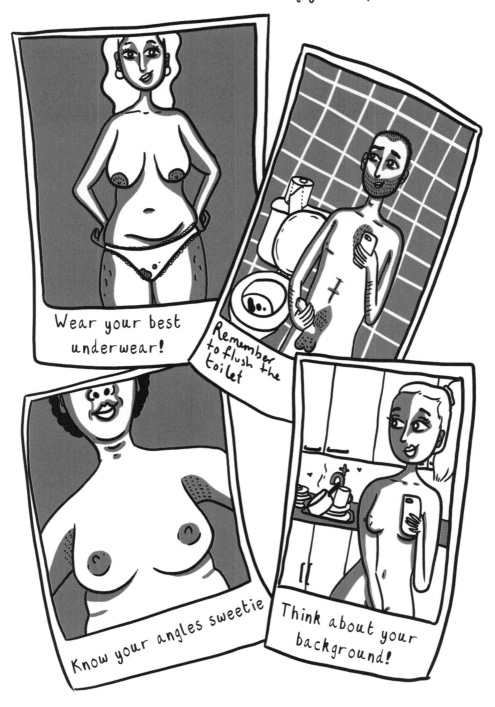

DATING

The bit where you find someone to shag.

Dating is horrible. Anyone who genuinely enjoys rummaging through the cesspit of humanity for months or years on end trying to find someone you can put up with enough to spend the rest of your life with is a psychopath.

Will, 29
Only message me if you too grew up rich enough to go on many skiing holidays.

MY MOST UNUSUAL SKILL IS... I make a cracking cup of tea... Ha ha!

Adam, 26
Looking for a girl to drop her entire life to go travelling with me. Or fantasize about it until she accidentally gets pregnant instead.

66 It's me! Your ex! And oh look I'm posing with your cat in my pics! 99

Being single is great. You have a whole ginormous bed to yourself (hopefully; if not, upgrade to a double, sweetie, you're worth it). You can masturbate as much as you like. You can cook yourself that weird meal that only you like. You can go out until 5 am and answer to no one, or leave a party at 9 pm because you're tired and everyone there is ugly. You can watch reruns of Masterchef all day long if you like (though maybe it's time to get over yourself and do some work, FLO, you have a book to write).

There are also such highs to being single. Flirting is so much fun. Swiping through dating apps with your best friend judging everyone's skiing pictures is hilarious. Actually finding someone who wants to have sex with you is an amazing feeling! Seeing someone naked for the first time is incredible. Everyone's naked body looks slightly different, it's like unwrapping a lovely fleshy present. And nothing is better than looking down on a boner that you created. Pure joy.

And then telling all your friends all your gossip the next day. Almost as good as the real-life boner (or metaphorical lady boner).

But then there are the lows. Going to a dinner party and being the only single person and everyone is talking about mortgages while this is the first meal you've had all weekend that you didn't just add boiling water to (look after yourself, sweetie, grill some fish fingers.)

Waiting for texts. Especially the texts that never come. Sending out a load of amazing one-liners on Tinder and getting nothing back. Oh, it's so painful.

Even when you do get laid the sex is of extremely variable quality.

And good sex is no guarantee they'll actually be a nice person too.

Dating is crap because it's a tiny percentage of pure joy and creating boners and a huge landslide of rejection. So how do you deal with the rejection? There are some things you can try to remember that might help make it slightly less shit.

It really is them, not you

So you're not getting matches on Tinder, or you came up to someone in a bar and they weren't interested, or you had a one-night stand that you hoped might turn into more and they never texted, or you went on three dates with someone and they ghosted you. These people don't really know you. And you don't really know them. They've had a tiny snapshot of you as a human, definitely not enough to decide whether you would make a great wifey for lifey for them. It's much more likely that something is going on in their life that means they can't handle you right now. They are not an expert on you. So don't dwell or what might have made them say "no"; it's impossible to know.

Try to remove your self-worth from the equation. It doesn't make you a worse person if you can't find anyone to sleep with right now. Get your self-esteem from other areas of your life. Ask your friends to be extra nice to you and invite you round for dinner and then bask in the glory of their love. Work out loads and marvel that you don't pass out at the end of the "Legs, Bums and Tums" class any more. Pour yourself into your work and try to be the bossest bitch you can be. Become the world-leading expert on Gregg Wallace's facial expressions by rewatching every Masterchef ever. Whatever works for you.

Remind yourself of just how many humans there are. SO MANY. And you have probably only snogged a tiny percentage of them (unless you're an absolutely massive LAD waaayyyheeyyy).

"Lad" is a gender neutral term from now on. Cos I say so.

Because of climate change there are not actually that many fish in the sea any more, but there are so many management consultants looking for wives. There will always be someone else you fancy out there.

Hi, I'm Tom

Hi, I'm Dave

Hi, I'm Matt

He might reply if I text him one more time!

He probably won't, babe.

If someone rejects you, just let them go. Don't chase them. Despite what teen movies have led us to believe, this hardly ever works. Even if you make them a whole Powerpoint about what a great girlfriend you'd make, they probably won't be into it. Put that energy into finding someone else to make out with.

GHOSTING

This is when someone you were romantically involved with stops replying to your messages or answering your calls. Getting rejected always sucks, however it's done, but ghosting is the worst way to gradually realize someone isn't into you.

Gary: Sorry, you're great but I'm not feeling this romantically.

One hour later:

Oh well.

You: Do you wanna get another drink this Friday?

//Seen:10:00

12 hours later:

It's possible he's dead and he lost his phone at the same time.

What should you do if you expect you're being ghosted? Give it 24 hours. Shit sometimes does happen, people lose their phone, they get busy at work, whatever. After that 24-hour grace period expires, confront them. "Are you ghosting me?" You're not crazy for feeling like shit if someone doesn't reply to your text for 24 hours.

If you have time to shit you have time to text.

If you can bear to, keep trying. Maybe the rejection is getting you down and you need some time out to learn to be happy alone, but I do believe it's worth it. For me at least, when you do actually find someone you click with, who actually likes you enough to have sober sex with you, and meet your parents, it is worth all the rejection. You can't protect yourself from getting hurt indefinitely; it will happen and you will get over it.

Let yourself enjoy the highs. Have guilt-free one-night stands. Join all the apps and then swipe left on everybody. Go out and talk to strangers. Flirt outrageously. Whatever works for you.

Humans are unpredictable, and some of them won't ever reply to your texts. Try not to dwell on that. Dwell on how fun it is describing a new willy or boob to your best friend the morning after.

FINAL THOUGHTS

Maybe you don't agree with everything I've said in this book. Feminism is something that's ever-evolving. Some things I say in this book might be wrong, or might age badly as we all get closer and closer to a gender-equality utopia. I'm just a regular gal who's read a few books you might not have read, spent far too long thinking about sex, and done a fair bit of field research let's not lie *wink* *wink* *wink*.

Even if you think this whole book is trash, I hope it's made you think, to examine the choices you've made in your sex life with a critical eye and to see that there are multiple ways to have amazing sex. Because that's what feminism means to me: choice. Feminism is the knowledge that you don't have to do what has always been done, or what some people might expect of you. You can challenge the status quo and blur the boundaries. Choose to be a stay-at-home mum or the CEO of some evil bank. Choose to sleep with as many people as you want to or decide that, actually, sex is overrated and you're gonna move to the woods and live alone studying the social system of some rare type of ant. Whatever rocks your boat.

Only you know what will make you happy and what kind of sex makes your head explode with pleasure, and I hope this book has opened your mind to more possibilities of what that looks like for you.

If you're not having great sex right now, or you're not having any sex and you wish you were, or you have had a traumatic sexual experience that you're still processing, it will all be OK. If you feel like you need to talk to someone, or even if you don't, do it anyway. Whether that's a professional, your best mate, or just your mum. Friends are way more important than lovers and they will get you through whatever you're going through. Also, don't worry about it. Sex isn't that great. So many things in life are better than sex. Like laughing and cake. You have your whole long life to have great sex - don't worry if it's not happening for you right now.

If you take one thing away from this book, make it to talk about sex more! Firstly, because it's super fun. And secondly, because it will make you have better sex. All too often we assume that everyone wants the same as us in the bedroom. Ask what someone wants, and if they don't ask you, tell them. More communication will only mean more people get to play out their secret kinky desires and less people experience something they don't want to do.

And then he put his mumble whisper mumble in my ....

Oh he's a keeper.

Yeah, there are still twats trying to block access to contraception, or make LGBTQ people's lives hellish; we don't know what effect free mainstream porn is having on the world, and many sexual lifestyles still carry a huge amount of stigma. But! I believe we live in the golden age for getting boned. Sure, we still have a long way to go, but I have so much hope. If nothing else, dildos are very affordable, next-day delivery exists and so does discreet packaging.

Thank you, Mr Postman, yes, more toys... for my cat.

NOTHING TO SEE IN HERE. DON'T OPEN MUM.

Acknowledgements

To my agent Karolina Sutton for being so enthusiastic about this idea and looking after it so well. To my editor Cecilia Stein at Penguin. It has been so great to have an editor that just fully believed in my vision. Your comments and encouragements have made this book infinitely better. To everyone else at Penguin, thank you for believing in my idea, and thank you for letting me have so much creative freedom. Big thank you to Luke Lewis, Robin Edds, Cate Sevilla and Tabatha Leggett at BuzzFeed UK for hiring me, training me, believing in me and giving me every opportunity to become the best writer I could be. (Extra thank you to Tabs for the help with the consent chapter.) To Hannah Jewell, the funniest person I know. Thank you so much for telling me my proposal was funny.

Thank you to my ex-girlfriend Lauren for always telling me I could do it.

Thank you to my parents. Sorry I wrote a book about sex, must be very embarrassing for you. But really, you only have yourselves to blame. What did you expect? Love you times a billion.

Thank you to all my friends. I am so lucky to have so many fun friends and I love all of you. A few people have been an exceptional support to me lately. To Emma, for texting me like I'm your boyfriend and talking about penises with me. To Tom - the last few months living with you has been such a delightful joy. To James, for living with me for five years!!! You are a constant source of laughs, support and love. To Jo, the wisest woman I know, the bestest pal a gal could ask for. I truly can't imagine my life without you.

Thank you to Brook Charity and the NHS for supporting my vagina through many years of adventure and many more years to come.

Further Reading and Listening

I read, watched, and listened to many things while writing this book. Here are a few of the things that had a profound effect on me and that I would recommend if you want to learn more about how to have a fun, feminist, sex life.

• Come As You Are - Emily Nagoski (I went to see Emily talk by chance and it changed my life. Her book is a whole new way of thinking about your sexuality. If you liked my chapters on non-concordance or desire, read it now!)

• Sex At Dawn - Christopher Ryan and Cacilda Jethá (Where I learnt everything I know about apes. If you're interested in non-monogamy, give it a go.)

• Shrill - Lindy West (A bible for learning to love your body and a funny book too.)

- Drawn To Sex: The Basics - Erika Moen and Matthew Nolan (A super practical and very accesible guide to having great sex. Also check out their blog Oh Joy Sex Toy)

• The Butterfly Effect podcast - Jon Ronson (A fascinating podcast series on the effect free porn has had on the world.)

• Savage Love podcast - Dan Savage (Dan has been writing a sex and relationship advice column for nearly 30 years and producing a podcast since 2006. You can't get a better picture of modern human sexuality than by listening to a few hours of his podcast.)

• On Sexual Consent, From a Woman Who Used to Be a Man - Meredith Talusan https://www.them.us/story/consent-patriarchy-and-aziz-ansari

• Not That Bad - Katie Anthony https://www.katykatikate.com/the-blog//2018/01/not-that-bad_15.html (a good look at the uncomfortable reality that different people define sexual assault in different ways.)